THE FEARFUL FIFTIES

The Fearful Fifties

A HISTORY OF THE DECADE

WRITTEN AND DRAWN BY

DAVID LOW

SIMON AND SCHUSTER
NEW YORK

The Fearful Fifties

A decade is perhaps too short a period in which to observe change in the pattern of life. The time permits novelty in detail but hardly any in the essentials of the design. So that, at a glance, the end seems not very different from the beginning except in emphasis.

Yet in that emphasis Progress marches. The pursuit of happiness (or whatever it is we are pursuing) has speeded up. And since the innermost secret of happiness, peace and hope, lies in a constant readjustment to ever-changing circumstances, a faithful limner—even in cartoons—of the past ten years could not but picture, as their salient feature, Man's quickened efforts to keep pace with the consequences of his own ingenuity, mechanical, scientific and political.

On January the first, 1950, we were fearful of the H-bomb, of the arms race, of scientists, of spies, of communism, of Russians and Chinese, of the dollar gap, the balance of payments and unemployment—and of fear itself. A dull thud from the direction of Soviet Russia was waking American generals up to the possibility that they might not have a ten-year lead over Russia in atomic missiles, as they had supposed.

Un-American Activities

In the United States a witch-hunt was galloping up against spies. In January Alger Hiss was on trial for perjury in denying he had been a communist, with horrific stories of a ghost typewriter, and of top secret microfilm found inside a pumpkin. American suspicion against scientists in particular was strengthened when, in Britain, a Harwell senior atomic bomb scientist, Dr. Fuchs, was caught and gaoled for passing bomb blueprints to Reds outside the British Museum.

Americans told themselves they had been quite right to keep things dark from the British. They decided their own chief atomic scientists, though loyal, might not be trustworthy either, and the problem of the time was how to get the best out of them without allowing them access to their own secrets.

Co-Existence

Relations with China and Russia were, of course, unfriendly. The Russians were arm-twisting the Western Powers by slowing down the railway from Berlin to Western Germany again. The Chinese communists were sore at America, first for keeping Chiang Kai-shek alive pretending to be still the Government of China set up at

Formosa as a strong-point in America's Pacific strategy. (The Chinese had no patience with the idea that the defence of San Francisco justified anyone keeping a gun on China's doorstep.) Second, because Washington therefore would not or could not recognise their new "People's Government" as China. Britain and France had done so but it had not brought them much good, because the P. G. had found an easy way of promoting trouble for foreign "imperialists" through the pseudo-"backdoor in the East". So there was fighting against Chinese-looking "rebels" in Indo-China, in Malaya, in Burma, etc. etc. . . . Stalin had a row with Tito of Jugoslavia, who insisted that his (Tito's) communism was more elastic than Stalin's, which was blasphemy; and Tito had another row with Italy about rights

in Trieste . . . There were pains in other respectable insides, too.
Belgium split about the return of King Leopold, so he abdicated;
and Greece had an election which did not suit King George, but he
"fiddled" it . . . It would be a mistake, however, to think of the
new decade dawning in a bank of clouds with no gleams of light.
A Commonwealth Conference sat in Colombo planning economic development of South-east Asia to offset the temptations of Communism
. . . There was much talk and writing going on of how to agree about
the Bomb, and the magic words "Control" and "Inspection" continued their shuttle service between Washington and Moscow . . .
At Geneva an interminable Council of Foreign Ministers' Deputies
chased one another around the mulberry bush . . . Trygve Lie,
General Secretary of the United Nations, visited Stalin personally in
Moscow to try to melt the cold war and came back with frostbite.

NATO, EDC

The New Year had a distinctly American look when President
Truman bluntly told the nations of Western Europe to get on with
their defence plans. Caught in the cold war, they huddled together

"TIME, GENTLEMEN, PLEASE!"

for warmth as scraps of paper blew around. The Brussels Treaty had
already bound five nations for fifty years to rush to the help of any of
their number if attacked. The North Atlantic Treaty, whereby the
United States, Britain and Canada pledged themselves to collaborate
in streamlining their combined defence resources, expanded into a
wider organisation (NATO) when the U.S. in January signed bi-
lateral treaties for mutual defence with seven other member States.
That might have seemed enough reassuring paper-work. But, to top
it, from the Council of Europe's Advisory Assembly at Strasbourg
came a revival of the old Briand idea of a European Army, the
European Defence Community (EDC). Other treaties had contemplated combinations of national troops for international purposes; but
EDC was to be a *supranational* army—a slightly different thing.
Everyone was most enthusiastic—until it struck the French that the
Germans would have to be included, and that would mean Germans
would have to handle arms. Statesmen could work out their solutions
as best they might, but French public opinion could not swallow that
one so soon after the war.

General Election

The British people voted at the General Election for more Fun. The Attlee Government, having filled a crowded page in the statute book, had run out of policy and popularity. The austerity imposed by post-war economy cost it all but a fraction of its majority. Attlee carried

on a tight-rope act, giving a new sporting interest to parliamentary life. There were few new faces in the Government, but very soon it was to lose two of its best men. The health of Stafford Cripps and Ernest Bevin was breaking up. The Government's domestic miseries of 1950 continued to be controls, wages claims, the cost of defence, the gap between dollar imports and exports.

Darkest Africa

Dr. Malan, Prime Minister of South Africa, wanted to take over the three Protectorates, Bechuanaland, Basutoland and Swaziland, but the British Government delayed because, according to the traditional

doctrine of Empire, South Africa seemed to be steadily evolving backwards. To worried idealists, the problem concerning the advancement of subject peoples to self-government was how to ensure that the freedom of democracy was not used as a stepping-stone to anti-democracy. South Africa was adopting segregation and permanent inferiority for original Africans as a national policy. And what, asked critics, could one expect of this policy, if not the eventual union of millions of blacks against a handful of whites in bitter race hatred?

Empire to Commonwealth

Hitler had been right when he predicted that a second world war would break up the old Empires. The French colonial system was cracking in Indo-China and in North Africa. There were rumblings underfoot for Britain in Malaya, Ceylon, Cyprus, Singapore, Egypt, the Sudan, West and East Africa. The mere presence of China, combined with the example of India, had encouraged subject peoples generally to seek "liberation" from Colonial Offices, and for long to come the air was to be thick with Asian and African delegates flying to Whitehall to arrange terms and measures of self-government. Empire had looked for a new *modus vivendi* and seemed to have found it in Commonwealth. But as Britannia retreated from "colonialism" the ex-subject peoples, remembering the past, could not resist

heaving half-bricks. "Emotional nationalists" wanted no attachment to Britain save favourable terms of trade, loans and the right to call the British names. In return they offered little more than a precarious respect for "interests" and the playing of the British National Anthem when visited by the Queen of England (who was understood to be also Queen of the Commonwealth).

'GAD! SOLD OUT TO THE NATIVES AGAIN!'

Korea

Point was given to peace talks when the armies of communist North Korea, without warning, drove into non-communist South Korea, a battle-scarred peninsula set up, because of its strategic importance, as an independent democracy by the United Nations. President Truman had learned the lesson of the old League of Nations in the 'Thirties. The United States which, naturally, had naval and air forces in the vicinity, moved in to resist the invaders. The Americans had appointed themselves advance agents of the United Nations, but their action was confirmed by the Security Council so quickly that the Russians missed

their chance for a veto. Troops of the French Union and the Commonwealth, who were busy nearby fighting bitter wars against Chinese
"rebels" in Indo-China and Malaya respectively, soon appeared as the
nucleus of a United Nations army. The North Koreans, with Chinese
reinforcements and Russian tanks and planes, had the best of it in
their first rush; but as troops and material arrived for the South, they
retreated to the 38th Parallel, where they had started from. President
Truman and his Secretary of State Acheson thought this might be a
fitting point for peace talks.

MacArthur

The President of South Korea, Syngman Rhee, disagreed. Rhee turned out to be just about the most quarrelsome "victim" ever plucked from disaster. Having the forces of several nations deployed on his premises, he was unwilling to waste them. He wanted to go after the stalled enemy and give him hell. In this he was backed up by the United Nations Supreme Commander, General MacArthur, who was said to be, with Chiang Kai-shek, cooking up a plan for invading the Chinese mainland through coastal points adjoining Formosa. Questions arose in the United Nations and opinion in the United

States came near the boil. Sides lined up. For a moment it was doubtful who was President—Truman or MacArthur. The former flew out to the South-east Pacific to settle the point with the latter. General MacArthur was recalled. Neither Truman nor Attlee nor the United Nations members associated liked the idea of being caught by the leg in an unpredictable war against China, when at any time they might need to deal with sinister happenings elsewhere.

Germany Rearms

Korea and Indo-China were object lessons in the Far East that made Europe aware of its own weakness. The birth of the European Defence Community seemed more likely to produce a family fight than an integrated army able to guarantee security against a surge of communism. Although it had been a French idea in the first place, no French Prime Minister appeared able to explain it so that it stayed clear and won approval in the Assembly. The idea of a European Army in which national contingents would be integrated and redistributed, that was understandable. But *German* contingents integrated and redistributed with Frenchmen—*pas possible, m'sieur*! The NATO defences remained painfully inadequate at about 17 divisions against 175 Russian; and even that was costing too much. Taxpayers were

asking what seemed the natural question: why should the victors of the late war, Americans, British, French, etc., pay for the protection of the vanquished, Germany? West Germany could not be left a vacuum in the defence system, but why should not it provide its own security? Everybody could see that it already had an oversized husky "police force" with a suspiciously military look. In anticipation of the completion of EDC, agreement had been reached with Dr. Adenauer and signed on the dotted line. According to him, his West Germans were reluctant to rearm at all, but he offered to persuade them—at a price: return of full sovereignty, equal status, and no deals among the Four Powers to be made at the expense of Germany without Germany's consent. Thus the master-mind installed himself as the arbiter of peace thenceforward. When he signed the EDC contract, France could do no less. Exchanges of rhetoric could still be heard off-stage about "never again suffering Germany to have arms" and "comrades in the defences of Western Union" as European statesmen left for home, supposedly to ratify a treaty. But the argument continued.

Russia Reacts

The rearming of Germany was just exactly what Stalin did not want. The object of all his foreign policies since 1945—the formation of a belt of reliable buffer States, the Oder–Neisse line detaching East Prussia to Poland, the blocking of "German unity" except under communist control—had been to keep Germany harmless and Russia

safe. After all, this bellicose neighbour had invaded Russia twice in one lifetime, killing 25 million Russians on the last occasion. Regarding the subsequent disharmony between himself and his former allies through a fatal transposition of cause and effect, Stalin was stricken comparatively dumb at what appeared to him to be a betrayal. The opprobrious adjectives and adverbs had become so hackneyed in Soviet progaparanda that "warmongering imperialist hyenas" was the best he could do. As a counter to NATO he gathered his satellites into a rival combination of "friendship, co-operation and mutual assistance" under the name of The Warsaw Treaty. To be on the safe side he had already begun to rearm communist Eastern Germany. When he saw the Americans were in earnest and General Eisenhower was arriving to take over the command of NATO, he looked around for his trick Peace Table.

Home Sweet Home

Against the world background the social scene in Britain during 1950 seemed almost cosily domestic. There were jibes at the "British Narrowcasting Corporation" because of its alleged deterioration in controversial matters . . . M.P.s returned to the House of Commons, rebuilt after its bombing during the war . . . Scottish nationalists pinched the Coronation Stone from Westminster Abbey . . . Peron doubled the price of Argentine beef and cut down our meat ration . . . Petrol rationing was abolished . . . An American rocket probed the upper atmosphere to a record height of 106·4 miles . . . Etna erupted . . . and Bernard Shaw's will was read with raised eyebrows.

Austerity and Self-help

Is it worth it? asked the British taxpayer when Chancellor Gaitskell told him that the defence programme would cost him £5,000 millions over three years. The likelihood that that would mean a pruning of the social services caused Nye Bevan to fly out of the Cabinet window. British production was already over 30 per cent more than pre-war, offset by a 45 per cent rise in the cost of raw materials. There had been a sharp rise in the cost of living but the Government, like those of other NATO countries, had accepted full rearmament. The United States was the richest, so naturally the other NATO members depended on her not only for economic but for military help. But the United States was calculating how much it could spend to defend Civilisation out of what it needed to spend to keep it worth defending; concluding that in future it would send fewer dollars and more encouragement to self-help. Mystic combinations of capital letters like ERP, OEEC, ECA, EPU, multiplied, understood to have something to do with mutual assistance.

Nationalisation

Despite their precarious majority the second Attlee Government brought forward one more nationalisation—of steel. The other three "nationalisations", however, remained arrested half-way at state capitalism, because the Government shrank from pressing on its supporters the second half—job evaluation and a national wages policy. Cripps had performed the miracle of a wage-freeze up to then, but Trade Union leaders, embarrassed by mutiny among their rank-and-file, could no longer hold back wage claims unless he limited profits. The Government thought this would discourage private enterprise in the mixed economy. The unions decided to stand firm on their capitalistic principles and would sell their labour for its highest price, nationalisation or no nationalisation. Socialism remained, like Christianity, an aspiration, something to be talked about but never tried.

Schuman Plan

The Council of Europe and its Consultative Assembly at Strasbourg, forerunner of a European federal parliament; the Brussels Treaty; the Benelux coal-and-steel pool; and perhaps even a European Army—these showed that the idea of Western Union had inspiring possibilities. New community projects followed, industrial, commercial and political. Talk had begun on the Schuman Plan for a wider coal-and-steel pool for all Europe and the establishment of a European common market with freely interchangeable currencies. Such notions would have made British grandfathers whizz in their narrow graves. Even their grandsons shivered. Prime Minister Attlee vaguely promised voluntary co-operation, but there had to be an open door and a rope ladder for the British, who loved fresh air. No supra-

SHOT-GUN WEDDING

national authority, thank you. From the beginning, the British Left
Wing (particularly, then, Ernest Bevin) feared that any such
authority, in Europe as it was, would have an anti-socialist majority,
and that might hinder countries like Sweden and Britain with
Labour governments from developing their policies; the Right Wing
feared disadvantages to "interests" and danger to Britain as banker
of the Sterling Area.

Peace, Imperfect Peace

When the communist North had appeared to be winning in Korea, and Soviet Russia had been invited by the United Nations to help restore peace, Soviet delegate Malik offered simple advice: expel Chiang Kai-shek's man from the United Nations and give his seat to a representative of the Peking Government; stop the Americans and let the Koreans fight it out. A Soviet peace offensive followed, against "aggressors". Prague promoted a Peace Congress to be held in

Sheffield to win popular support for Soviet peace proposals. These unfortunately left the Soviet's relative superiority unimpaired and the non-communist West's inferiority confirmed. Visas were questioned and the Congress went home. Then the preparations to establish NATO in Europe inspired new efforts. Russia invited the Western Powers to a conference on Germany but the suggestion was lost in fog. A delegation from China led by General Wu travelled to the United Nations to explain that the Chinese in Korea were not troops but "volunteers". There was doubt as to whether, not being "recognised", he should be invited to sit or to stand, and the party broke up when he was asked to admit that China was an "aggressor". At last, on the proposal of Soviet delegate Malik, peace talks on the war in Korea began at Panmunjom.

"WHAT'S HE GOT UP HIS SLEEVE?"

NO CHEST FOR THE MEDAL

Vietnam

When the French returned after the World War to Indo-China to carry on their Protectorate of Vietnam where they had left off, they found the seat of State occupied by Ho Chi Minh, a communist-nationalist with an army of irregulars, who had installed himself as President after the collapse. The French looked around for a big personality to put against Ho, but could not find one in that disunited background. Finally they decided to recall playboy ex-Emperor Bao Dai from the French Riviera and set him up with plans for a rather bogus independence within the French Union for Vietnam, Cambodia and Laos. A miscalculation. The nationalists were not tempted because Ho Chi Minh had already roped them all into his camp, leaving only the pro-French, and these split immediately into two more factions, one for Bao Dai, the other against. Whenever Ho picked trouble and the war flared up, it was evident that he, like other communist war-lords in those parts, was supplied and rein-forced by China. Korea all over again. After long wearing months the war at last became more than the French had bargained for. They complained to their allies that they could not fight in South-east Asia and build up an army in Europe too.

General Election

The Tories returned to power, headed by the evergreen Churchill. The Churchill Government was committed to abolishing Austerity and restoring Private Enterprise. But it made no change. The financial climate being more severe than ever, owing to a temporary recession in the United States, Austerity continued. The Tories had realised that the Welfare State and full employment were fortifications to the capitalist system rather than otherwise, and they quietly appropriated these ideas to their own Party policy. They left the nationalised industries alone, with two exceptions: the nationalisation of steel was revoked and replaced by "voluntary" regulation under the National Steel Federation. Similarly, they "freed" haulage from nationalised transport to be run for profit, leaving railways to be run for service on the unprofitable routes. The Ministry of Health went on as before, to the accompaniment of bitter cracks about free teeth for the British Medical Association to gnash at politicians.

An Englishman's Home

1951 for the British was lightened by an Occasion and a sensation. The Festival of Britain opened in London, an architect's holiday that would have gladdened the heart of Prince Albert, with its Skylon, Dome of Discovery, and Fun Fair . . . Burgess and Maclean disappeared from the Foreign Office, turning up later in Moscow, to the puzzled fury of the Establishment . . . Britain's first jet bomber whistled across the Atlantic in 4 hours 40 minutes . . . There was a marked increase of gambling . . . Newspapers went up to 1½d. . . . The foundation stone of the British National Theatre was laid on the London south bank, where it remained until someone had it removed . . . and zebra pedestrian crossings came in.

Revolution in Egypt

After a flurry of politicians the Sphinx spoke and Egypt had a revolution. Amorous playboy Farouk skipped out of history into lurid private life, leaving a group of Army officers waving the flag of nationalism. The "front" for this revolution was General Neguib, a popular figure among the Angry Young Men of Egypt who blamed the corruption, nepotism and political rottenness of past régimes for the humiliating defeat of their army in the Palestine war. They did not accept the end of that war as final and still blocked shipping bound for Israel through the Suez Canal. Neguib was reassuring to Eden but when the British attempted to protect Canal installations from rioters they became Public Enemy Number 1. "Out with the British!" shouted the Cairo mob.

The King is Dead

King George the Sixth died in February at the age of fifty-six, in the sixteenth year of his reign. His eldest daughter Princess Elizabeth, who was in Kenya at the time, was proclaimed his successor.

The Gap

"No one is going to keep the British Lion as a pet" said Santa Churchill, decorating the Christmas tree with a good thick sprig of Austerity. The year 1952 found Butler, new Chancellor of the Exchequer, fishing for tiddlers in the Gap between dollar imports and exports. American orders were hard to catch because America was restricting imports, too. Big payments had to be made soon to the United States and to Canada. There was a slump in textiles. When Butler presented his budget, it cut food subsidies. Prices and wages slid up the inflationary spiral.

THE GAP

Apartheid

In South Africa the Supreme Court of Appeal ruled that the Act whereby coloured voters were placed upon a separate vote register was invalid, thereby shooting a large hole in Dr. Malan's Apartheid policy. Malan decided that he would fix things so that the Courts would be "protected" from the "danger" of testing acts of Parliament, by depriving them of any say in such matters. Furthermore he would send no more reports to the United Nations, because they seemed to be set upon imposing "unrealistic ideological shackles" on South Africa.

"WHAT BUSINESS IS IT OF YOURS? ANYONE WOULD THINK YOU WERE WORLD OPINION"

"NO INTERFERENCE" IN SOUTH AFRICA

Oil and Tears at Iran

A picturesque character resembling a pained parrot came up in Iran as Prime Minister, Dr. Mussadek. He began boldly by announcing his intention to get on with nationalising the oil industry, and forthwith took over the assets of the Anglo-Iranian Oil Company at Abadan. British Foreign Secretary Herbert Morrison and Richard Stokes found negotiations with Mussadek were peculiarly difficult, because when opposed he wept copiously and took to his bed. As well he might. The powerful Company set itself to obstruct his selling the oil to third parties; and with neither the power to exploit the oil nor the accustomed revenues from the Company, he had a problem.

"THERE, DEAR. NOBODY
WANTS TO LEAVE YOU OUT"

Sphere of Responsibility

In August ANZUS, the Pacific Security pact between Australia, New Zealand and the United States, came to life. Opinion in Blimp circles, already disturbed by the tip Butler had given the Dominions not to look for loans to hard-up Lombard Street, but to try Wall Street, was shocked at the absence of Britain from the membership. Were the Dominions in future to be considered as lying within the American "sphere of responsibility"? Was the United States trying to join the Empire or vice versa?

" GO IN AND BRAND 'EM, COWBOY "

McCarthyism

The witch-hunt against Reds in the United States became fantastic.
Senator McCarthy, chairman of the Senate Investigating Committee,
employed his own staff of investigators and was untiring in smelling
out spies and traitors. Prominent scientists, public servants and film

stars lined up to have their good names smirched. Americans in the United Nations service who had been in contact with foreigners were bidden to investigation. The State Department was left in no doubt about the danger of mixing with the British Foreign Office. Mr. Truman was undoubtedly a Red. Even Roosevelt and Churchill were suspect for having associated with Stalin at Yalta. The Senator was prepared with a strong "purge" policy for the incoming President.

Ike

General Eisenhower was elected President of the United States. "Ike" was universally liked and had all the glamour of having "won the war", but he was new to politics. It was feared that he might turn out to be an innocent in the hands of the machine politicians. Anxious eyes of world statesmen, so dependent on American policy, looked apprehensively at his choice of John Foster Dulles to be his Secretary of State and, in effect, the chief spokesman for Democracy against Communism for the next ten years.

Family Circle

British small talk about events in 1952 was in general tinged with gloom. The first British atom bomb was exploded, at Woomera . . . General Ridgway took over Eisenhower's command at NATO, not Field-Marshal Montgomery as the British had wistfully expected . . . The U.S. Alaska Air Command landed an airplane on the North Pole . . . After a revolution lasting 77 minutes Batista made himself President of Cuba amid tumultuous popular rejoicing (in the customary Cuban style) . . . Seretse Khama, chief of the Bamangwato tribe, married a white wife and was detained in England until his brother chiefs in Bechuanaland got over their Colour Bar.

Stalin Dies

A wondering world read of the Doctors' Plot reported from Moscow. Stalin had been ill and nine Jewish doctors had been arrested for plotting "to shorten the lives of Soviet leaders by injurious treat-ment". In February the beloved Russian leader died from a stroke,

and members of the Central Committee were explaining their relief at having got rid of him at last. Changes followed. Malenkov and Beria were rivals for the succession. Malenkov became the new Chairman, Khrushchev, hitherto little-known, was soon Secretary General of the Party. Stalin's pets in government service were fired, stories circu-lated of his tyrannical monopoly of personal power and Pravda called for collective leadership in future, instead of personal decisions. The new passwords were "Collectivity" and "Monolithicity".

Beria

This view was not unanimous. Beria, an "old Bolshevik", Stalin's Number One and Minister of Internal Affairs (including Secret Police) was noticed to have slipped away to Georgia where he was assembling personal support for grabbing power. In July he was invited back to Moscow, where he was quietly shot and tried for treason. The British wanted to take advantage of the change of rule as an opportunity for a new approach to Russia, but Eisenhower's new Secretary Dulles of the United States was mistrustful, so much so that some said he suspected Stalin's death to be a cunning ruse.

Coronation

The Coronation of Queen Elizabeth II took place in June with traditional pomp and pageantry. The nation spent £1,000,000 on its celebrations, which, considering the state of its finances, testified to the popularity of the Monarchy. But when publicists of the Establishment wrote and talked overmuch of "a new Elizabethan Age" and strove to find some parallel, preferably romantic, between the age of aristocratic oligarchy and the age of popular democracy, they only provoked criticism of the Court advisers who "presented" Monarchy in the trappings of the mediaeval past instead of in a manner befitting leadership of a great present-day Commonwealth. News arrived simultaneously of the successful climbing of Everest by the Hunt Expedition, starring Hillary and Sherpa Tensing, which was greeted as a Happy Omen for the new reign.

"WE BROUGHT YOU OUT TO ENJOY YOURSELF, AND ENJOY YOURSELF YOU SHALL!"

Mau Mau: State of Emergency

Haunted by a fear that Dr. Malan, Prime Minister of South Africa, might get there first with a take-over bid, the Colonial Office decided to hurry on with plans for a Central African Federation of Northern

IN DARKEST KENYA

THAT'S TORN IT

and Southern Rhodesia and Nyasaland. It called a conference to
settle details of "partnership". The Africans had ideas of their own
and did not attend, so the view of the European settlers and their
supporters was accepted that Africans were politically immature and
their minds should be made up for them. It was soon evident that the
opinion was mutual. The Africans had no faith in the professed safeguards against the suppression of their nationalist aims. Protests led
to opposition, opposition to violence, which was followed by an
undiscriminating suppression of "unlawful societies" and "subversive
elements". Mau Mau, a widespread murder movement, flared up
in Kenya chiefly among the Kikuyu tribes. Brutality called up
counter-brutality to a tragic climax.

Agonised Re-Appraisal

All these months gone and still the European Army was waiting at
the church. The French Assembly could not make up its mind to
ratify EDC. It had nightmares: first, that the Americans might back
out and go home when they had a European Army in going order;
second, that the British might desert them, the French, and leave
them alone with, and outbalanced by, the Germans; third, that the
Germans might play up and break away out of control. France's
unreadiness to commit herself to such perils was increased by vague
hopes that it might be possible after all to make a deal with the new
Russia. But Secretary of State Dulles had had enough. He did not

"LOOK OUT! HE'S MAKING AN AGONISED
REAPPRAISAL"

forget that the State Department had asked for EDC and arming the Germans in 1950 because these measures were considered necessary for the defence of Europe. It was getting hard, said Dulles ominously, to keep Congress interest from swinging away from Europe to the Far East; and harder to resist separating the agreements with Germany from EDC. In short, said he crustily, if certain people around here don't get on with their ratifying, the United States may have to make an agonised re-appraisal of her own basic policies. That

GROWTH OF LITTLE FRITZY—A CAUTIONARY CARTOON

was enough. The laggards quaked at the prospect of losing American help. The pace speeded up. EDC dropped dead, the Brussels Treaty was expanded to accommodate all the nations concerned, as a political

MAKING SURE OF ADENAUER

instrument to keep the European idea alive. It was renamed Western European Union and it became part of the NATO defence system. All the military arrangements were concentrated within the NATO framework, and Federal Germany became a member of NATO with fitting safeguards and controls.

Nehrutralism

Although Nehru could be tough about the Kashmir question with
Pakistan, he often bent over backwards to keep friendly with
communist China, and deplored attempts at collective security among
the small Asian peoples, especially if they involved Pakistan. Nehru
was credited with the ambition of creating a Third Force to hold a

world balance of power between the giants, America and Russia. Not so, he protested. All he wished was to get as large an area as possible of countries which did not want to encourage any tendencies to war.

Vietnam

The Americans were paying much of the cost of the war in Indo-China and avoiding actual participation. But when Dulles took over the State Department at Washington the view narrowed. He balanced the risks of French defeat, leaving bare to the blast Malaya, Indonesia, Burma, Thailand, etc., against those of a World War III with China and Russia, and decided meanwhile on a policy of threats. British Foreign Minister Eden thought things had gone so far that the best hope of saving something from the wreck lay in negotiations. It suited Eden when Molotov proposed a Five-Power conference, including China, to "reduce tension" generally. After a fight in the backroom, Dulles promised to sit down with the Chinese. But first he had to put things right for the French. The division in Vietnam over the reinstatement of Bao Dai was now so deep that a sardonic critic suggested Ho Chi Minh should be called in to mediate. What the French wanted, explained their Prime Minister Bidault, was military and air support—not advice from Dulles or the United Nations on how to run their politics, thank you. (Their mistake, thought their friends).

BIDAULT:
"MERCI, M'SIEU. BUT WE DEFINITELY DIDN'T ADVERTISE FOR A LAUNDRESS"

LINE IN INDO-CHINA

"YOU WANNA KNOW WHATSA MADDER WIT BRITISH FILMS? YOU WON'T GIVE YOUR WHOLESOME YOUNG WOMEN THE ENNERTAINMENT THEY LIKE ... "

STATE OF THE CINEMA

Home Front

The cinema film industry defended itself against the menace of television by a burst of technical improvement in the way of larger pictures, distributed sound and three-dimensional effects with polaroid spectacles . . .

Newspapers prospered on selecting suitors for Princess Margaret, especially on stories of a Royal romance which, with the intervention of the Archbishop of Canterbury, came to nothing . . . Russia exploded its first hydrogen bomb . . .

PALACE GUARD

Experts of public art galleries were embarrassed at the boom in the values of famous paintings as assets for investment. It seemed too risky to buy cheap works, for how could one know if a painting were good except by waiting to see if its price went up to £30,000?

A gang of ghosts attempt to crash a fashionable art auction. It is explained that painting can only be appreciated by rich people. The intruders are ejected and retire muttering.

Free and Open

For many months Soviet Russia and the Western Powers had been talking (sometimes at the tops of their voices) about EDC, NATO and how to make a regular peace treaty with Germany. Now at last Molotov, Dulles, Eden and Bidault met for a Berlin Conference on the "German Question". Dulles wanted to hold "free and open elections" throughout both Eastern and Western Germany as a prelude to forming an all-German government; Molotov wanted to form the all-German government, and *then* hold the free-and-open. But Dulles (and Adenauer) did not recognise the Eastern German leaders as a government until they had been elected in free-and-open. Molotov said he had no objection to free-and-open if he could be sure who was going to win. He could not understand why everybody was so set on free-and-open. Hitler had come into power as the result of a free-and-open. . . . The Western Powers went home depressed.

"But don't you offer any alternative?
"What, and risk losing the election? Are you kidding?"

"'FREE NAVIGATION'? THAT'S _ME!_"

Suez

In Egypt, General Neguib had served his turn and was supplanted by his "strong man", Colonel Nasser, as Chief of the Revolutionary Council. Nasser had fixed ideas. He dreamed of uniting all Arab peoples in one nation. He refused to be integrated in a new pact of mutual security, the Bagdad Pact, because he thought that would hinder his purpose. He was moved by a bitter hatred of Israel, which, in his view, had usurped Arab Palestine and, worse, had ignominiously beaten the Egyptian armies when they had sallied forth to right the "injustice". Nations that had in the past helped Israel, particularly the British, came in for his furious denunciation. After tortuous negotiations Britain and Nasser struck a bargain on the Suez Canal base: complete withdrawal of British forces, with exceptions and under conditions, within twenty months; and Nasser to recognise that the Canal, while part of Egypt, was of international concern. But British Foreign Secretary Eden remained apprehensive, and General Sir Brian Robertson, the C-in-C, had doubts about the scowling passers-by being there to drop in for a cup of tea.

HOLIDAY SEASON IN SUEZ CANAL

Lamb bites Dog

The tide turned for Senator McCarthy when he began to probe beyond the legislative part into the executive part of government in the United States. Vice-President Nixon denounced McCarthy's "reckless talk and questionable methods"; and since some doubt had arisen as to whether Eisenhower or McCarthy led the Republican Party, he felt it necessary to assure the world that Eisenhower was the unquestioned leader. In March Adlai Stevenson criticised the President for not opposing McCarthy's "character assassination" of respectable citizens he suspected of communism, reproving "a party divided against itself, half McCarthy, half Eisenhower". McCarthy's own investigating sub-committee was encouraged to investigate matters involving his staff. Finally the condemnation of the Senate extinguished the Senator.

"JUST A LOT OF UN-AMERICANS "

In the image: "Communist try for victory in the Tongking area" · "American Impatience"

Geneva Conference: Korea

A shaky armistice had been achieved at Panmunjom after three
years of wrangling broken by a short renewed war and salted by
imaginative propaganda accusing the Americans of dropping diseases
from the air. A Five-Power political conference of all concerned met
at Geneva to make a peaceful settlement. The war in Indo-China,
being "under the same management", was dealt with at the same
time. The conference opened badly because since the United Nations
did not recognise China, China would not recognise the United
Nations. Chou En-lai was subtle, Molotov tough and Ho Chi Minh
shifty. The conference failed over Korea, but that war simmered
down at last to an exchange of prisoners which itself became a kind
of secondary war—with Syngman Rhee in the middle threatening to
take on India and the United States with one hand.

" PEACE HATH HER VICTORIES, EH, COMRADE ?"

THE PEACE-LOVING PEOPLE

Geneva Conference: Indo-China

The Indo-China side of the Conference began even more unhappily. With negotiations under way, thought the political strategists, it was imperative that France's bargaining position should not be weakened by her losing ground in the fighting. On the other hand, American and French war experts dreamed of how that position could be strengthened by a resounding victory. Bad went to worse and on the eve of the Conference news came that the soundest of the French troops were heavily outnumbered and undergoing a major defeat at Dien Bien Phu. The Americans were so deeply shocked at the crumbling of the French and the victorious march of communism that Eisenhower and Dulles came very near sending planes and joining in, conference or no conference. Decision hung on the British. The British thought this would be asking for World War III and said "No". (Dulles no doubt remembered that "No" when Eden wanted the United States to do something for *him* in the Middle East two years later—but the Americans had always thought the Far East was more important than the Middle East.) Vietnam was partitioned, the bigger part going to Ho Chi Minh and his communists. The power of the French Union in the East accordingly shrank and the United States had to be satisfied with Ho's promises of no more "liberating" of mythical "resistance movements" in Laos and Cambodia and all-Vietnam "free" elections. An insulting time was had by all.

"GOSH! I HOPE THE OLD MAN ISN'T GOING TO USE LIVE AMMO...."

Cyprus

A copious beard and black canonicals were destined to become all too
familiar to the British when a new and picturesque figure entered the
world scene, Archbishop Makarios. While the Western nations had
been consolidating the Bagdad Pact, a kind of modified NATO of the
Middle East, Cyprus had been developing a patriotism of its own. It
called for ENOSIS, union with Greece. But the strategic importance

"D'YOU THINK IT CAN BE OUR BAGGAGE THAT DOES IT?"

"PERFECTLY WILLING TO GO YOUR WAY— IF YOU GO MINE"

of the base at Cyprus had grown for the British since parting with the Suez Canal zone. The Colonial Office suggested self-government to go on with and sat down to write a constitution. Makarios spurned the offering and began to make the island too hot for the British. The situation was complicated by the unwillingness of a Turkish Cypriot minority to be ruled by Greeks or even by Greek Cypriots. Soon three-cornered murder-around-corners was under way.

ANY MORE FOR THE SKYLARK?

SEATO

After Indo-China, Dulles and Eden immediately got to work on another collective defence system on NATO lines—the South East Asia Treaty Organisation, SEATO. Britain, the United States, France, Australia, New Zealand, Siam, Pakistan and the Philippines signed the treaty. To Bidault it was like bolting the door after the burglary, too late to save the French Union; but France signed. India would not. In any case Dulles, who had taken a dislike to Nehru, said that if they wanted India he would propose Formosa. Nehru, who was busy agreeing on the Five Principles of Co-Existence with his guest to Delhi, Prime Minister Chou En-lai of China, deplored SEATO as likely to stop the "trend of peaceful thinking".

"YOURS, MES AMIS. I ALREADY CARRY ARMS"

"— AND IF ANYONE ASKS YOU WHAT YOU'RE DOING HERE, TELL 'EM YOU'RE SELLING TICKETS FOR THE POLICEMEN'S BALL."

Policeman of the Pacific

On the principle of never allowing Washington a night's sleep, China tried a third probe into America's will-to-resist. Forces of the Chinese People's Government heavily bombarded Quemoy and the Matsus. The bellicose anti-China lobby in the United States Congress, coupled with MacArthur's well-known idea of invading the Chinese coastal ports with Chiang Kai-shek's troops from Formosa, had not passed

IMPORTANT OBSERVERS

unnoticed by the communist leaders of Peking. They decided to scotch
that plan by capturing the line of islands which could be used as
stepping-stones between the mainland and Formosa and announced
the impending "liberation". The presence of the American Seven-
teenth Fleet, ostentatiously minding its own business but flying from
its masthead a new treaty of mutual security with Chiang, probably
had much to do with discouraging the enterprise. The shelling died
down, the People's Government had gained Tachen Island and lost

its enthusiasm. The diplomatic exchanges involved were held by American liberals to present an opportunity for peace talks of a comprehensive kind with China's People's Government. But the difficulty was what to do with Chiang.

WEAKNESS OF DEMOCRACY IN BLUFF POKER

WHAT SHALL WE DO WITH OUR CHIANG?

Lord ("outrage") Hailsham and
Graham ("Golden Mustard") Sutherland meet at
the Tate Stadium to decide, in the customary
manner of settling art disputes, whether
the Churchill portrait is a masterpiece.

Many Happy Winstons

First among British domestic pre-occupations of 1954 was Winston
Churchill's eightieth birthday, which was celebrated with general
rejoicing, including an immense gathering of political notables in
Westminster Hall who presented him with a brilliant portrait of
himself by Graham Sutherland which was disowned by the Philis-
tines as "an outrage painted in golden mustard". Other momentous
events: Roger Bannister ran a mile in 3 minutes 59·4 seconds . . . the
Independent Television Authority was set up after long and earnest
debate on the corrupting influence of Commerce upon channels of
communication . . . the "Dynamos" football team from Moscow came
to play soccer with Wolverhampton Wanderers—"cultural diplomacy"
slightly marred by a tactless bungle over hotel accommodation; a

ceremonial visit of Tito to London . . . and a Flying Bedstead which
flew straight up at Farnborough. During the year the traffic crush
had steadily worsened, which prompted a sarcastic suggestion that
the Transport Ministry should forbid "horseless carriages to enter,
leave, stop or move during the hours of 12 p.m. and 12 p.m.". . .
a deplorable growth of American influence was noted in religion,
glamour, styles, comics, gum, gags, songs, music and dancing; but, to
balance things, America was much admired when the United States
Supreme Court ruled out racial segregation in school as uncon-
stitutional.

Post-Stalin

Changes in the State and Party machinery in Soviet Russia suggested that a new hand was spring-cleaning the "old Bolsheviks". Malenkov slid down, Bulganin flew up, Zhukov made a brief reappearance and vanished, followed by Kaganovitch. Party Secretary Khrushchev told the Supreme Soviet that there would be a high priority for heavy industry, as against consumer goods and housing. This, and the new anti-Stalin line, caused basic-policy trouble among those who put the improvement of life in Russia before the strengthening of communist power in the world.

MANAGERIAL REVOLUTION IN RUSSIA

EARLY SPRING CLEAN

Inflation

In February Britain had another balance-of-payments crisis. Life had been one chronic state of unbalance and recurring crisis ever since the

"YOUNG MAN, IS THERE ANYTHING TO STOP
THIS LIFT FROM SHOOTING THROUGH THE ROOF?"

"DUNNO, MUM. I JUST PRESS THE BUTTONS."

PRICES

UP, UP, UP.

end of the war. This time it was due partly to a worsening of world trade abroad which nobody could do much about, and partly to inflation at home. Parties had their traditional cures for inflation: the Tories, deflation, risking some unemployment; Labour, planning, with wider spread of wealth. But both policies would have had to make productive investment the priority, and both would have been unpopular in an election year, so neither was pushed. Chancellor of the Exchequer Butler assumed the rather worn mantle of Cripps-austerity and dealt with the situation by raising the Bank Rate and instituting a mild "credit squeeze". Micawber waited for something to turn up.

"IN THIS BUSINESS IT'S NOT ENOUGH TO BE GOOD — ONE MUST ALSO BE CAREFUL"

SSH !

Grand Old Man

Churchill resigned the office of Prime Minister. He had governed too long, but the British people still revered him as the man whose spirit saved them from the Nazis. As he tiptoed out of office (the Press was silent in a newspaper strike) he could reflect that his monument lay all around him. Of his continuing influence on the nation's affairs, it need only be said that his last Government contained nine of his relatives—sons-in-law, cousins and connections by marriage. A striking evidence of democracy in action.

Mr. K.

The scene had changed in Moscow, where Mr. K. went out to demonstrate changes for the better since Stalinism had been abolished. He opened a few windows in the Iron Curtain for Western tourists and American journalists; put forth a peace plan and disarmament proposals and accepted an invitation from the Western Powers to a Summit meeting. On the way he made a pacifying visit to Tito in Jugoslavia, and invited Chancellor Adenauer of West Germany to visit Moscow. Adenauer was less distant than before because his disputes with France about rearming and the Saar had been settled

HOLE IN THE IRON CURTAIN

THE FAMOUS
PALAIS
'SPHERE'

LOW
Geneva
1955

in the framework of the new institution, Western European Union.
British Foreign Minister Macmillan had been assiduously massaging
the rigid Mr. Dulles to a more flexible attitude. All being prepared,
in June the Big Four met at Geneva for a Summit.

Summit

The Geneva Conference of Heads of Government "represented a success for the peace-loving peoples" in that statesmen saw what each other looked like, which eased their tension. Germany, disarmament, security and contacts were discussed but without conclusions. It was agreed that even if the meeting had achieved nothing, it was the best nothing that had yet been achieved. The Heads left directives to their Foreign Ministers, who duly met later and deadlocked between the extremely unlikely and the highly improbable.

TEMPTATION OF ST. ADENAUER

THE
H-BOMB
ARGUMENT

BOTH (together) " ISN'T IT TIME YOU WERE GIVING UP?"

ANOTHER CO-EXISTENCE PROBLEM

Science

Dull summer weather probably brought to a climax a conflict between conscience and mundane expediency. A declaration of eminent scientists, including Bertrand Russell and the late Professor Einstein, called on mankind to renounce war, saying that the use of nuclear weapons would "quite possibly put an end to the human race"; to which equally eminent politicians replied that Survival and the Conditions of Survival were inseparable, constantly posing problems and involving risks. Nightmare discussions arose about the possible genetic mutations that might result from the fall-out of strontium after bomb tests, one view being that one mutation which resulted in an Aristotle, a Leonardo, a Newton or an Einstein might well outweigh ninety-nine that led to mental defectives. Horrific rumours spread of scientists experimenting on an inexplosive bomb which would just quietly disintegrate the universe; and of the U.S. Army's chemical corps getting on with another new weapon to incapacitate an enemy without killing or permanently injuring him. In the same time President Eisenhower had presented new proposals for the peaceful use of atomic energy, under United Nations auspices; and had announced plans to rocket a satellite through space to circle the earth. At Jodrell Bank the world's largest radio telescope was completed and able to "watch" such wonders.

'It might become imperative "before acceptance" to enquire into the applicant's history of exposure to radiation"

Boy Geigers Girl

RADIATION ROMANCE

'In such a world, diminished fertility and a shortened life-span "might not be altogether to be deplored"'

Arms Deal

In the Middle East the test of friendship was the supply of arms, and so long as the United States, Britain and France controlled that, they thought they could control the situation. But Israel remained ringed with Arab enemies, all resentful of the 1949 Armistice, chief of these being Nasser of Egypt, who never stopped proclaiming to his Arab League that "a state of war still existed against Israel". Despite the efforts of Dulles and U.N. Secretary Hammarskjöld, demarcation-line "incidents" and village raids multiplied with equal ferocity on both sides, particularly in and around the Gaza strip. At last the United

" SORRY, M'SIEU, CAN'T HEAR A WORD FOR THE NOISE OF THE TRAFFIC "

"WHY DON'T THEY ASK ME WHAT RUSSIA THINKS?"

Nations patched up a cease-fire. But in September Nasser told the world that since no one else would sell him arms, he had arranged to get them from behind the Iron Curtain—from the Skoda Works of Czechoslovakia. The Western Powers were depressed. This was notice not only of more savagery but also of Soviet Russia's intention to fish in the waters of the Nile.

Family Album

It was an emotional year at home. Vast crowds assembled at Harringay Arena, scene of famous championship fights, to seek spiritual uplift under the direction of Dr. Billy Graham, American evangelist . . . A strike stopped London national newspapers long enough for people to find, rather uneasily, that they could live without them . . . Another round in the battle of the sexes was won when the Burnham Committee upheld the principle of Equal Pay for women teachers . . . The A and H dress lines came in and demonstrated once again that a pretty girl can survive any hideous garment. By comparison the Edwardian styles adopted by "Teddy boys", who came into prominence for the first time, were almost aesthetic. Nevertheless the sartorial return to the past by corner-boy youth was deeply resented by the middle classes, to whom it was unseemliness amounting to misdemeanour (which seems unnecessarily insulting to our grandfathers—but then the original Edwardians did not carry bicycle-chains or flick-knives, only umbrellas).

"THE FIRST THING TO DO IS TO CLEAR AWAY ALL THAT JUNK AND PLANT POTATOES—AND NOT LYSENKO POTATOES, EITHER"

CHANGE IN USSR

1917-1957

"TO ANOTHER 40 YEARS OF COMRADSHIP AND UNITY"

Cult of Personality

The Stalin legend had already been punctured, his statues removed, and streets re-named, but it took Khrushchev to finish the job. In a long speech at the 20th Party Congress he ruthlessly exposed the dead dictator's excesses and mistakes and deplored his "Cult of Personality". (It was generally agreed that the cult of Khrushchev's Personality was quite a different matter.) Stalin's "short history" of the Communist Party, basic Party text-book, would be revised and a new Party programme would be drawn up. This would stress peaceful co-existence and the betterment of relations with the outside world. Anyone who didn't like it would be "unmasked". One more of Stalin's old hands, Molotov, was sacked. Too much Personality.

Makarios

In March Archbishop Makarios of Cyprus sat at the Seychelles counting sea-shells on the sea-shore. He had been deported by the British when Cyprus had gone from bad to worse. The difficulty had been that Cyprus lay in the Mediterranean and was strategically an essential part of any Middle East defence system of NATO or the Commonwealth. The British could afford self-government but Makarios demanded self-determination, a very different thing. The arrival of a new Governor, Sir John Harding, with an armful of olive branches, had been met by bomb-bursts, provocative Athens radio and appeals from Turk-Cypriots who had wanted no part of ENOSIS and had the most casualties so far. The Governor tried to

BIRDWATCHING AT THE SEYCHELLES

BLIMP IN CYPRUS

counter with curfews, bans, proscription and soothing private talks for the Archbishop with the Colonial Secretary. No good. So they deported the Archbishop, and then they had nobody to negotiate with.

ROCK 'N' ROLL

"THE U.N.? HOW MANY TANKS HAS *IT* GOT?"

High Dam

Playing one side against the other paid Nasser in favours and flattery. Dulles thought that stability in the Middle East depended on his goodwill, so he (and Eden and the World Bank) offered to put up the money to build Nasser's pet project, the High Dam at Aswan. Nasser accepted, but made no promises. Israel's relations with her Arab neighbours, not only Egypt but also Jordan and Syria, had deteriorated into intermittent warfare. Israel's Premier, Ben Gurion, trusted nobody; he believed that Nasser's armies were gathering at Gaza to

attack, so he sent up artillery and attacked first, just in case. The
United Nations worked hard, but Hammarskjöld could find no
"climate of peace" in Israel. No one could decide what should be done
nor how to determine the aggressor if real war came. As Nasser's
dealings with the Iron Curtain became thicker, his threats and abuse
rose to crescendo. Dulles hesitated before his bellicosity and then told
him that the United States had thought again and would not advance
the money for the Dam. Nasser furiously kicked back by proclaiming
that he had nationalised the Suez Canal and would get the money
from its revenues.

THE COLOSSUS OF SUEZ

K. and B. Visit Britain

After a preliminary call from Malenkov in March, Khrushchev and Bulganin came on a goodwill visit to Britain in April. Their sensational arrival was only slightly dimmed by rival attractions in the shape of

publicity concerning two famous beauties of the screen, Marilyn Monroe and Grace Kelly. The occasion cleared up the question as to whether the Soviet system had evolved to the Left or the Right. Khrushchev obviously was at ease with the barons of industry. "If I lived here I would be a Conservative", he confessed, less humorously than was supposed. On the other hand his only exhibition of anger was at a Labour Party dinner when someone asked him about

GLAD HAND

Individual Liberty. Otherwise relations with the guests were
cordial, save for a frogman who wrote a dirty word on the keel of
their battleship.

Emotional Nationalism

"To have independence is not enough; one must also *look* independent" should have been the slogan of some of the ex-dependents of British colonial government. Certainly as one by one they lined up to demand the key of the street from Britannia, it seemed they had to prove their maturity by kicking the old girl downstairs. Even when British troops had withdrawn from the Sudan in 1953 after general agreement, the Egyptians (who were trying to detach the North from the South) had found plenty of Sudanese stooges to curse and accuse Britannia of trying to detach the South from the North . . . In the case of British Guiana in 1953, she had been guilty, said Chief Minister Jagan, of culpable interference and tyrany. Guianese

"DON'T GET LOST IN THE SUGAR, OLIVER"

PASS, CASHBOX! HALT, POWERS OF DARKNESS!

Ministers had been planting a few totalitarian experiments of their
own among the sugar canes, and were about to reap bankruptcy and
rampant violence, so the Colonial Office had put back the constitutional clock until the growth of an informed public opinion and
independent trades unions . . . When it came to Cyprus, contempt
and bombs were the reward of Britannia for continuing "to assist
the people of Cyprus to develop their own political institutions
and to proceed in an orderly and peaceful manner towards self-
government" even if she had to drag them by the ears . . . When

"EMOTIONAL NATIONALISM"

" I wonder why children never want
Grandma to depart through the front door
but always long to kick her down
the back stairs ?"

Malta turned up for notice, the Maltese were abusive and thankless. The position of Malta as a fortress made it difficult to "liberate". It was too small and lacking in resources for independence, anyway. The answer to Malta's economic troubles, said Prime Minister Dom

Mintoff, was Integration with the United Kingdom. And Integration meant Equivalence, which meant a standard of living for the Maltese equal to that of the British. Malta would make the best contribution it could and Britannia should pay up to balance the budget, to create capital works, new industries and employment. Britannia accepted and wanted to discuss Integration questions, particularly religious Equivalence, but Mintoff wanted the financial part settled first. The new constitution and all that stuff could wait. It became painfully clear that Malta's answer to her economic problems was Make Britannia Pay. Britannia hesitated. Mintoff, with loud disgust, went home and stood his policy on its head . . . Contumely dogged Britannia to Singapore. Negotiations in 1956 to establish an internally self-governing "State of Singapore" to replace the Colony of Singapore might have opened in an atmosphere of mutual congratulations. Instead Chief Minister Marshall so violently expatiated on what Singapore would *not* do to suit the external responsibilities of the U.K. to the Malay Federation (which Singapore sought to join) that it seemed his co-operation could only be counted on for pushing Britannia into the docks . . . Ceylon was as touchy. Ceylon's independence had been attained in 1948 under conditions of post-war pleasantness and prosperity. But by 1955 the high price of rice and the language problem brought in a new government determined to tidy up. It demanded the return of the naval and air bases. Britannia promptly acceded, which annoyed the Ceylon government, which had expected profitable negotiations. The government demanded the Ceylonisation of executives and staff posts in agriculture and industry. That drove away overseas investors, which diminished the revenue, which raised the taxation, which irritated the government still further. Britannia, the government decided, was altogether too crafty, wouldn't stay put. Ceylon must consider becoming a republic.

S-S-STILL IN THE SA-SA-SADDLE

De Mortuis

Khrushchev's exposure of Stalin's sins and mistakes "relaxed" the peoples of the satellite states, especially Poland and Hungary which had both suffered cruelly from Russian greed and bad management.

Anti-Stalinism quickly developed into anti-Sovietism. In both countries the old Ministers identified with Stalinism were sacked, political prisoners released, popular heroes lately shot for treason dug up and given State funerals. There was more freedom of speech, the Press wrote more freely, and in both countries new leaders were hailed, one from prison, one from exclusion, eventually into seats of power—Gomulka in Poland, Nagy in Hungary.

THE LINE

Suez Canal

Nations using the Canal protested that it should be run by an inter-national body, and Britain and France took a resolution to that effect to the Security Council of the U.N., but Russia blocked it by a veto. Tanks began to move. Israel invaded Sinai. Indecision. Eden saw Nasser as another Hitler, out to expand and rule the entire Middle

"CARE TO ADD A NEW INSTALMENT, M⯑ SECRETARY ?"

REFLECTIONS IN A CANAL

East, his thumbs already on Britain's communications and oil;
Mollet, Premier of France, saw Nasser as openly hostile in France's
North African wars and feeding her enemies with Skoda arms;
Israel saw an intolerable menace to be confronted before it was too
late; Dulles, apart and caught in complicated calculations (not for-
getting the United States elections) thought Eden exaggerated
Nasser's potentialities and saw him, Nasser, as a piece in an involved
game of chess he, Dulles, was playing with Soviet Russia, the important factor in the situation which he hoped finally to move to his
own advantage if someone didn't push the table over. Dilemma for

Eden: should Britain rely on the United Nations and patiently await developments, hoping for the best? Or should he take a lead out of the American book and "do a Korea," go to war for the U.N. in advance, seeking confirmation later? That, of course, would be risking the Atlantic Alliance, the United Nations and the sympathy of the Afro-Asian peoples. The Russians would certainly make use of warlike action both coming and going—first, by increasing help to Nasser, and second, by advertising it as a precedent for their own designs. But. . .

"Bring up our left to repel Egypt, wheel our right to throw back Israel, advance our centre to hold up America, Russia, Yugoslavia, Nationalist China, Persia, Cuba and Peru........"

NIGHT IN THE DESERT

REPAIRS AT MOUNT SINAI

Eden and Mollet decided. British and French troops landed and, with the Israel forces, put the Egyptians to flight. Victory... followed by inglorious humiliation. World condemnation was so vast as to dismay Eden and Mollet. Only the Biggest Powers could do things like that. British and French armies withdrew as soon as possible, leaving the United Nations to pick up the political pieces.

Poland and Hungary

Moscow worried about the satellites Poland and Hungary. They seemed to have turned away from Stalinism not to Khrushchevism

WORKERS' COUNCIL

"NO HONOUR, NO PITY, NO HUMANITY?"
"NOTHING BUT THIS"

COMRADESHIP IN HUNGARY

but towards Titoism. Top Soviet leaders visited Gomulka and saw he was a shrewd politician, that he appreciated Poland's geographical position and, at a pinch, would co-operate with Russia for defence. So they let him alone . . . All might have gone as smoothly for Hungary had there not been a bad harvest. The starving people blamed Russia for everything. Throughout the country excited youthful crowds carried Imre Nagy to the top on a six-point programme of which the first point was Russia Must Go and the second Denounce Warsaw Pact. Nagy, who was no realist like Gomulka, was pushed to proclaim that these two points would be adopted and

"GOOD-BYE, COMRADE— I'M OFF NOW. I'M ORDERED TO VOLUNTEER TO GO AND DEFEND SOMEBODY'S RIGHT TO LIVE HIS OWN LIFE WITHOUT INTERFERENCE"

"PEOPLE'S DEMOCRACY"

carried out forthwith. The Soviet troops began to move *out* by one road; but *in* by another with bombers, tanks and artillery. In ten days they had beaten the revolt flat.

CROCODILE TEARS

IF IKE SNEEZES—

Ike's Fitness

After his stroke in 1955, a dreadful interest in President Eisenhower's health was taken not only by American politicians but by the outside world as well. Democratic governments abroad could hardly contemplate a "constitutional vacuum" in the United States without feeling ill themselves. Through the Press they became as well acquainted with the President's interior as with his exterior and anxiously followed his processes day by day.

FAMILY GROUP

Day After

Anthony Eden retired from politics, ill, soon after the Suez débâcle. A statesman of talent and judgment in his long past, he had proved in his Big Mistake a valuable lesson—that the Go-it-Alone policy was played out in the modern world. His successor Harold Macmillan met Eisenhower at Bermuda and patched up the alliance. France and Britain reassured the willing United Nations Assembly and withdrew their armies, Israel following under protest; the U.N. sent an international emergency force to keep the peace, and a salvage fleet to clear the blocked Canal. President Eisenhower, evidently conscious of the contribution made by the ambiguity of the United States to the inglorious story, decided to clarify the future by pronouncing the "Eisenhower Doctrine": the United States was prepared to use its armed force to assist any nation or group of nations against armed aggression by any country controlled by international communism.

Deterrent

The original concept of NATO was of a shield of 60 well-equipped divisions contributed by member-States; but as one member-State after another cut its quota again and again on grounds of expense, NATO plans were pared to the bone and the gaps in man-power had to be filled with tactical atomic weapons. When Britain abolished conscription and Defence Minister Sandys announced yet another drastic cut in man-power contribution, he suggested yet more "atomic combat teams". NATO C-in-C Norstad was aghast at the example set to the others. If all members declined to maintain conventional forces in convincing numbers, withdrew behind their own frontiers and abandoned Europe to be a nuclear battlefield, any little squabble might automatically become a world war. Trip-wire defence? Who would trip?

"YES, BUT WHO ARE WE ECONOMISING FOR? US OR THEM?"

United Arabs

Nasser felt cocky over his Suez "victory", warmed by promises from the Iron Curtain and ready to go ahead with his scheme of a one-Arab-League-State. He assembled at Cairo for conference Saud

*"NO, NO—CAN'T BE DISTURBED—
HE'S WRITING THE 'NASSER DOCTRINE'"*

CONCENTRATION AT CAIRO

ARAB AND HIS STEED

of Saudi Arabia, Qwatley of Syria and Hussein of Jordan. Iraq and
the Lebanon did not come, because they were scared of Nasser's
communist backers and they had both publicly welcomed the
"Eisenhower Doctrine". The conference deplored Israel, Britain and

"IS THERE A DOCTRINE IN THE HOUSE?"

ON THE FENCE

France as "imperialist aggressors" and it declared, somewhat incongruously, for positive neutrality. Saud (who was said to spend half his oil money on palaces at home and the other half on corrupting his neighbours) had just leased an air base to the Americans, and wasn't so sure; neither was Hussein who didn't like communism. All that was profoundly unsatisfactory to Nasser, who saw that changes would have to be effected. Warming up Cairo radio he called for riots and demonstrations in the reluctant states and was busy disintegrating Jordan when the American Sixth Fleet was sighted off Beirut, which

WATCHING THE SITUATION

POKER GAME IN THE PERSIAN GULF

cooled that off. Then he used Syria, by now almost a Soviet stooge, as a jack to upheave the pro-Western régime in the Lebanon, but it wouldn't stay upheaved. Annoyed, he tried to dig a hole under Libya; and set fire to Iraq. When Jordan and Iraq in self-defence formed a rival Arab Union with Saud complaisant, Nasser seemed to be achieving unity at the wrong end. It was necessary to show results. He therefore proclaimed to the world the federation of Egypt and Syria in the United Arab Republic; and after a week of parades and pomp, settled down to wondering whether he would touch Moscow or Washington for the next loan.

Common Market—Free Trade Area

The "six" countries of the Coal-and-Steel Community got on with the next stage of European integration. A plan for the Common Market emerged aiming at abolishing trade barriers; making rules to prevent distortions in national life arising therefrom; and fully developing European resources. A Council, a Commission and an Assembly would co-ordinate and fix harmoniously problems of conversion, readaptation and investment. Agriculture had to be an essential feature of the Common Market, and that scared off the British with their subsidised uncompetitive farmers. A dilemma arose for the British. If they joined they would have to stand Imperial Preference on its head and turn over their responsibilities in the Sterling Area. If they did *not* join they would be in a disastrously

HERE COMES THE BRIDE

" LOOK WHAT I MADE OUT OF THE SPARE WHEEL"

bad bargaining position because they could never compete in Europe when its productive power was efficiently organised. So they suggested another idea, either as an alternative or as a kind of fifth wheel to the Common Market 'bus: the Free Trade Area. It differed in that Britain and other like-minded countries would exercise their own controls, and remove all tariffs with Common Market countries while retaining tariffs with third countries outside OEEC. In that way Preference, the Commonwealth, the Sterling Area and the farmer could all be preserved.

Blip Blip Blip

The Russians launched the first artificial world satellite "Sputnik".
The world thought it a great scientific achievement, but to Moscow
it was a symbol of the superiority of "communist science" over
"capitalist science". Four weeks later they sent up another rocket

with a live dog inside it, and "Little Lemon" soared to world fame as a worthy addition to the Pantheon of Soviet heroes, before disappearing in space. The Americans had foolishly advertised their own attempt to launch a satellite and when it failed gloom descended. Loaded with inferiority complex, their scientists retired to the laboratories to go one better.

H-tests continue in Russia.
A new bomb to end all
bombs is fired straight
from Mr. K.'s big mouth.

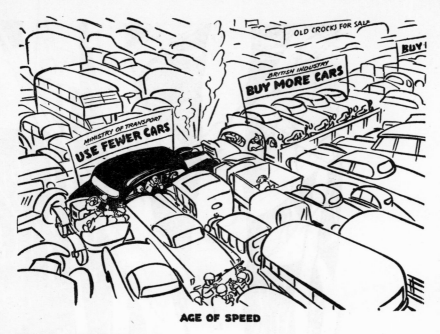

AGE OF SPEED

British Background

In Britain 1957 marked an advance in the Windfall State and a slump in national morale . . . There was a shocking rise in juvenile delinquency . . . Fantastic "pools" prizes and an increase in gambling generally tempted the Government to issue Premium Bonds, alleged to combine thrift with luck . . . An economist discovered a way of saving by more spending. The prosperity promised thereby would raise the standard of living, for those that could afford it . . . At the beginning of the year the Egyptian trouble temporarily solved London's traffic problem by causing a shortage of oil; but the car industries continued to expand and the conflict between road space and vehicle multiplication achieved an accident total for the year equal to estimates for an A-bomb explosion . . . London parks were officially opened to be resting-places for cars between manslaughters.

BABES IN THE JUNGLE

Accra Conference

"World-government" "One-worlders" had doubts about the wisdom behind the new enthusiasm for the balkanising of Africa into a string of militant nationalisms, possibly with war for supremacy in the end. They looked with interest on the first Conference of Independent African States. But Kwame Nkrumah, who had called the conference and used Ghana as the inspiration to achievement, declaimed brotherhood and pan-Africanism with West African federation as a start. The assembly revealed Africa to be not a big solid mass as it looked on the map, but a collection of little countries with widely differing ways of life and governmental systems ranging from ancient autocracy to modern pseudo-democracy. The idea of nationalism dominated the occasion. Neither Moscow nor Washington could have derived much encouragement, for the conference, with Tom Mboya in the chair, was very much on its guard against "outside influence".

De Gaulle

In France the "policy" since the war had been to catch up inflation by raising wages, and Frenchmen could not understand why they should not go on like that for ever. Faced with bankruptcy, they blamed the politicians, as usual. The direct cause of the flare-up in May was the war in Algeria. The Generals and the French-Algerian settlers insisted on top priority; and the war was costing the earth and seemed to be getting nowhere. After a rapid succession of govern-ments torn between wishing to fight the war and to negotiate the peace, the Generals revolted, took the law into their own hands, set up a Committee of Public Safety in Algiers, sent an ultimatum to Paris, cursed the politicians and shouted for General de Gaulle the patriot. In response de Gaulle offered to take over. An imminent national explosion forced the politicians to give way. De Gaulle elbowed aside the Constitution and consented to be persuaded to take

JOAN AND THE VOICES

CONTINUATION OF THE FRENCH REVOLUTION

charge with a government of all (non-communist) parties, holding special powers for six months. The Fourth Republic, having reduced democracy to an absurdity, had guillotined itself.

Iraq

When an officer-led revolution flared up and the ruling group were murdered in Iraq, it seemed to Nasser that the victory must be his and his United Arab Republic efforts were paying a dividend. A slight mistake. When the dust cleared General Kassem and Colonel 'Arif were in charge, with no discernible programme but a general notion of "popular rule" and "liberal" reform. By the time purging had finished and popular ferocity had died down, Kassem found he had a full-time job balancing the mixed races, religions, ideologies, groups and tribes of his disunited community. Unfortunately his Deputy Prime Minister 'Arif had a talent for simplifying things to the point of trouble, so Kassem's balance finally came to be between

Nasserism and Communism. Kassem saw no reason why he should tie
himself to either, so he played off one against the other and vice versa.
If anything he objected most to being integrated with that lot of
camels at Cairo, so to get rid of his encroaching top Nasserites he
assembled his communists; and when the latter completed their
assignment and got above themselves he strove to revive some
Nasserites long enough to get rid of his communists. The last part of
that operation met with less success, for the communists had dug in.
After a year, however, the power was still uncertain, the juggler still
had several balls in the air and still proclaimed his independence.
The only point of agreement between Nasser and Kassem was hatred
of Israel. Otherwise their personal recriminations kept the Middle
East awake. To Nasser Kassem was Arab Public Enemy No. 1, the
traitor who was opening the gates of the Arab World to Communism;
which was pretty rich since he, Nasser, had Cairo full of Soviet
experts and his own pockets stuffed with Russian credits at the time.

NO PRIVACY IN THE MIDDLE EAST

Notting Hill

The race conflicts of South Africa, Kenya and Little Rock seemed to have come to a focus on London's doorstep when young hooligans began to beat up West Indians at Nottingham and Notting Hill. But these insalubrious districts were not representative of Britain. Notting Hill had always had street gangs used to fighting among themselves when there were no "foreigners"; and it was no favourable place to attempt the integration of numerous coloured immigrants with their own strange customs. The birch, the cat and similar traditional correctives had just been abolished, and a few exemplary prison

PROBLEM FOR THE WELFARE STATE

sentences did not prevent further widespread outbreaks of vicious ignorance enjoying the fun of violence. Incitement by Fascist crackpots to race-hatred brought the danger of rival strong-arm race groups. More police moved in and things cooled off . . . until next time.

SIESTA ON THE SPIRAL

Unofficial

Democracy was a basic principle of Trade Unionism, but so was Solidarity. That made a headache for the General Council of the T.U.C. when it had to face more and more "unofficial" strikes by

BULLDOZER

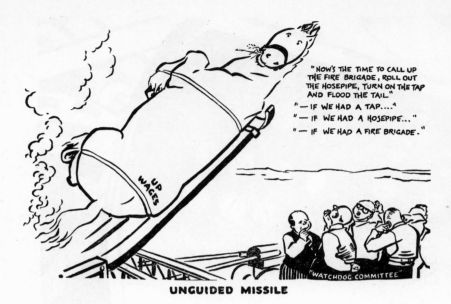

UNGUIDED MISSILE

ET TU, COUSINS

mutinous groups of workers who kicked the pants of their union leaders and tore up the book of rules, often for trivial reasons of pride or jealousy. The evolution of small craftsmen into technicians at sensitive points in the complex machine of modern industry was said to give shop-stewards an obstructive influence beyond their proper function. Since the aims of the latter, when they did not actually smell

THREAT TO THE OLD HORSE

of disruptive communism, were on a lower, more selfish level than those of the "constructive advance to a just society" of Labour policy, the T.U.C. was left constantly feeling its own pulse to see how far it had been weakened against the inevitable risks of the advancing press-button age and a fall in the demand for labour that could not be cured by strikes.

THE HORSE'S MOUTH
" REMEMBER, HUGHIE, LESS ECONOMICS
AND MORE FULL EMPLOYMENT, SEE ? "

Money

In 1957 the British Treasury and the Bank of England passed sleepless nights about Inflation and the Currency. All the measures taken since then to keep the pound sterling both stable and flexible had not been particularly effective. The "credit squeeze" had only made people annoyed at being put to the trouble of raising the wind elsewhere. Capital issues control had been futile and restricting the supply of money irrelevant, hardly touching the problem. The wizards of finance, before they tried anything else, decided to employ the

"I MAY BE OLD-FASHIONED BUT I
PREFER GOOD OLD BRAIN-WASHING"

TOUR OF THE BANK VAULTS

Radcliffe Committee to examine the consequences of their actions
and report in precise statistical terms. There was a shivery interim
during which the pound sterling followed the devalued French franc,
the German mark and most other European currencies into dollar
"convertibility" (but the pound followed only to a limited extent,
because the wizards remembered that last time they took that road

THE BOOM IN CLEAN SHEETS

they fell on their faces). After two years the Committee reported. It was not the pound that had been at fault, it was the world. The pound had had to do what it could against the compulsion of inter-mittent pressures from within and without; direct controls had fitted the 'Fifties, restriction of hire purchase and control of fixed invest-ment had been right and proper, particularly in the public sector; internal policy should certainly be internal, and external policy should be, if anything, more external. Quite, quite. The City was blameless and the Bank would remain as of yore, except that the Chancellor himself, instead of the Governor, would proclaim changes in the Bank Rate, which would no doubt impress foreign speculators;

"WHAT'S THAT SLIPPING SOUND? THE BRAKES?"
"CAN'T BE. THERE AREN'T ANY."

CURRENCY JOYRIDE

RESCUE SQUAD IN THE CITY

it would be wise for the Governors of the Bank to spend more on research so that they could know more about the workings of the monetary system. If we all had confidence in continued prosperity and the nation did not go bust, all would be much the same in the 'Sixties as in the 'Fifties.

Progress of Civilisation

The year 1958 showed Man coping with his own ingenuity. ZETA (Zero-energy thermo-nuclear assembly) was uncovered at Harwell. . . . The United States launched the first atomic submarine . . . Soviet Russia and the United States played darts at the moon . . . and the Hula Hoop came in . . . Public Opinion Polls had now become a regular feature of journalism, horrifying in the revelation of popular ignorance about public affairs . . . a Hire Purchase boom began which gave

THE ART MARKET

the ex-Oppressed Worker who did not know what to do with his Brighter Future an opportunity to mortgage it back to capitalism . . . Pasternak was awarded the Nobel Prize for Literature, and the Ignoble Prize by the Soviet Writers' Union, who thought his "Dr. Zhivago" should have had more heroes . . . Well-known old paintings brought fabulous prices at art auctions, and no doubt the ghosts of the painters reflected that even if they had had to exist on the smell of an oil rag in their lifetimes, it was nice to think they were accepted when dead as sound lock-ups for capital in 1958 . . . Field-Marshal Montgomery's Memoirs triggered off generals the world over shooting their mouths in a continuation of World War II . . . a litter act came into force just after August bank holiday without any apparent lessening of dropped orange peel or cigarette cartons.

Tourist Season

"Russia is not in East Germany to play skittles", said Khrushchev, making a cunning move in Berlin to force the Western Powers into a Summit conference. Rather was the game in Europe suggestive of Alice-in-Wonderland chess played with human beings. Statesmen began to move. Mikoyan moved to the United States. Macmillan moved to Russia. Adenauer gave warning of moving in several directions without leaving his square. Ulbricht moved to Moscow.

" DOCTOR 'DEMOCRACY', I PRESUME "

He told me that privately he was a good Tory like me, but like me he has his "Ike" to think of.

He said Moscow was full of crackpot Socialists who preferred a higher standard of living to hard work. Most of them were shut up, but there was still one behind every curtain.

He didn't mind A-bomb inspection at all. He would even undertake to inspect Russia himself personally to save everybody trouble.

He sympathised with us about Nasser. He'd had trouble with Nasser himself. Nasser was put up to it by a bandit named Tito.

Why this fuss about Berlin? He was just withdrawing Soviet forces from foreign countries. Wasn't that what we were always asking?

The session ended with his bursting into what he alleged was a fusion of both our National Anthems.— "Gossave our Gracious Hammeransickel"

MOSCOW RECONNAISSANCE REPORT

ARTFUL MIK'S GOODBYE

Khrushchev moved to Albania, then to Poland and was about to move to Scandinavia, but thought twice. The Foreign Ministers moved their chairs at Geneva. Vice-President Nixon moved to Russia. President Eisenhower moved to Germany, then to France, then to Britain. Finally Khrushchev, to intense excitement, moved to America. . . . When Eisenhower was asked by a journalist what all that activity had been about, he said they had wanted a negotiating Summit, but seemingly they could only get an exploring Summit. No one would move backwards.

DETROIT

Cars for the rich. Workers can afford only two each.

WALL STREET

No capitalist hyenas in sight. Recession obviously in progress

LINCOLN MEMORIAL

Diversionist comrade misled by that bit about people not being able to live half-slave half-free...

YOUTH

Disorderly bands armed with banjos and trumpets infest the dance halls, corrupted by American influence

EDUCATING NIKKY

Leaping Progress

The decline of Stalinism in Russia did not exactly please Mao Tse-tung in China. Mao compared Khrushchev to Stalin to the former's detriment, and implied that China was now the ideological leader of the communist bloc. To prove it China would achieve communism first. China would do this by "piecemeal industry" through "communes", whereby the Common Man would hand over his private

PRIVATE LIFE IN PEKIN

WITH ONE EYE ON BIG BROTHER NEXT DOOR

property, receive back a share of the "Four Necessities of Life" and be put to work where he was most needed. An era of "Leaping Progress" was announced. The first figures of achievement in the leap which were fantastically high and later had to be severely cut, were won at the cost of landing in such a bog of popular unrest and Party dissent that the Government was shaken and felt it necessary to gain "face". Formosa or Korea were "out" because the United

States was too ready. But one could still put the bite on unsuspecting friends. So Tibet, China's "independent" associate, was invaded, occupied and picked clean. Khrushchev was embarrassed, but in the sacred name of solidarity he had to stand (without enthusiasm) behind Mao. When Chinese soldiers neared Tibet's traditional frontiers with India, however, he began to run around in circles. He had interests in Asia, too, and he needed Nehru's goodwill. Furthermore, the Chinese were renewing their links with their former province, Outer Mongolia, now a Soviet satellite.

JUST AN OLD INDIAN CUSTOM

JUST AN OLD CHINESE CUSTOM

African Sunrise

During the 'Fifties British successes in painless transference of self-governing power to colonies and dependencies much outnumbered their fumbles. Libya, Singapore, Malaya, Ghana, Nigeria and the West Indies stood well against British Guiana, Cyprus, Malta and Nyasaland. As the decade ended Africa narrowed down to Nyasaland. The 1953 Act which created the Central African Federation (Northern and Southern Rhodesia and Nyasaland) provided for a conference to review its constitution in 1960. Black spokesmen of Nyasaland had never liked the idea of being cooped up in a government with the white settlers lording it, because they thought that would mean the end of any chance of their ever governing themselves. The whites would never agree to sufficient increase in black African political representation. Of all the alternatives offered, the only one the Nyasas liked was withdrawal from the Federation. The other two parties to the Federal Government, the Rhodesias, strongly objected. Nyasaland had potentialities to be developed with white

AFRICAN TROUBLE SPOT

resources of the Federation, they said, but alone it was not viable. It was short of administrative talent and capacity for self-government. The comparatively few educated young men had little contact with the vast mass of innocent fellow-Africans in the villages. Self-determination would give those villagers "democracy" which would be disguised dictatorship, which might be good or bad, but could be worse than Western "colonialism", said the Federal Government. Put like that it seemed to the "innocent Nyasaland villagers" not so much an invitation to partnership as to a plan for arrested political development. To make their dissent clear they resorted to riots and violence. A state of emergency was declared in Southern Rhodesia and "security forces" were despatched to keep order. A sharp conflict

flared up. The Government said that their action in taking and using
emergency powers and arresting African Congress leaders, including Dr.
Banda, was fully justified because of a supposed murder plot to
massacre Europeans. 11 people died and 79 were wounded—all black.
No European was killed. Bad was made worse by two tragic bungles:
Nkata Bay where 20 Africans were killed apparently because of a
misunderstanding; and Hola prison camp in Kenya, where 11 Mau
Mau detainees were clubbed to death. The white residents of Kenya
were no doubt surprised at the horror and indignation with which
all this news was received in Britain. Even moderate opinion began
to feel there might be something in the bitter words of Nnamdi
Azikiwe that these tragic struggles arose from "the fear of the
white minority that political consciousness among Africans would
deny them their privileges in Nyasaland". Mistrust of the Federation's
treatment of its non-whites increased. It led naturally to the sending
of the Monckton Commission and to the subsequent visits of the
British Prime Minister to see for himself, and feel the "new wind
blowing through Africa".

"IN THE NAME OF AFRICA (AHEM!) WELCOME!"

Miracle at Cyprus

Greece and Turkey felt that the Cyprus trouble was drawing them
back into the old pattern of enmity, but in a different world, in which
they would probably need one another. The Prime Ministers did not
think the emotional titivations inherent in ENOSIS were worth even
what remained of the Bagdad Pact; so after their Foreign Secretaries
had quietly fixed things at Zürich, Prime Ministers Karamanlis and
Menderes met and came out with the headlines of agreement. Thence
to London, where, with the co-operation of the Third Party, Britain,
a settlement was beaten out whereby both Greek and Turkish
communities of the island would share in government and allowance

"PERSONALLY I THINK WE SHOULD TAKE A RISK"

"A KIND OF MIRACLE" *says FOOT*

would be made for Britain's minimum strategic needs. Whereupon all concerned emerged from the shadows to be photographed with the beard of Archbishop Makarios, the Father of His Country. "It is a kind of miracle", said Sir Hugh Foot, the last Governor-General. All, that is, except Grivas, the *homme fatal* of EOKA. You can't campaign for ENOSIS with somebody who doesn't want you, so he melodramatically retired from politics and returned to Athens. Finding leisure irksome he re-emerged a few weeks later with blueprints for a new chapter of trouble, starting from the other end, taking over the Greek State and demanding the ENOSIS of Greece with Cyprus. But everybody was bored and preparing to get down to the job of framing a constitution in which there would be enough stumbling-blocks, goodness knows.

End and Beginning (1)

The decade was ending in an atmosphere of guarded optimism in the West. Four Summit meetings in 1960 were promised by Khrush-chev on Berlin, Germany, nuclear tests and disarmament—provided that at the appointed times Russia was still interested in agreements on Berlin, Germany, nuclear tests and disarmament, which to some observers was a pretty big "if". Signs that Russians often played their foreign policy as moves in a complicated struggles among themselves for power within the Kremlin, restrained over-confidence. No solutions were yet in sight for the fusion of the two Germanies. The end of the "tourist season" had improved personal relations all round, but nobody had parked his guns in the cloak-room. Mr. K. on return to Europe had made a quick trip to Albania to see

Dr. ADAMANT:
"OK! SO LONG
AS NOBODY THINKS
I AM THE BALL"

HUDDLES

"PEEP-BO!"

about a base there in case the NATO Powers took advantage of the
improved good feelings over Cyprus to plant a base in Greece. The
Russians' threat (which had started the runaround) to upset the
Four-Power position in Berlin by turning their own functions there
over to the East German Government, thus forcing the Western
Powers to deal with the latter, was less tense without a deadline,
but still hung on the air ominously. The conference at Geneva on
banning nuclear tests worked hard all around the subject but never at
it, endlessly discussing tests under water or in the sky; when inspection teams should call—not when something had exploded but at

"NOW LET US SEE YOU UNLOCK IT"

prearranged intervals like the gas-man or the TV service, always subject to veto; and a bright Russian proposal that, to avoid un-pleasantness, countries should each provide their own inspectors—Russians to inspect Russia, Americans to inspect America and so on. Mr. K. suddenly proposed total and complete disarmament, but would not be pinned down to any formula or procedure. Later he said he would not wait for the others but would demobilise a third of the Russian army right away, filling up the gaps that were left with nuclear missiles. When reminded that all, including himself, had a conference working at how to abolish nuclear missiles, he said well, why don't they get on with it? . . . It seemed that the nearer the mountaineers got to the Summit, the further it receded.

End and Beginning (2)

Times changed, but not if Dr. Adenauer could help it. At 83 after ten years as Chancellor he had come to think of himself, personally, as the bastion against further Soviet encroachment into Europe. He felt too many misgivings about the unreliability of possible successors to retire. Everything was arranged for him to pass on to honoured repose by making himself President, but at the last moment, to the consternation of his ambitious lieutenants, he declined and instead tightened his hold on the helm. No-Unity-Before-Free-Elections and No-Scrapping-Arms-Before-General-Agreement were permanent banners so far as he was concerned; and, though that was not the time to open it up, the correction of the Oder–Neisse frontier with Poland was still unfinished business. So long as the Powers disagreed, Federal Germany was "sitting pretty" as a virtually guaranteed State. But Dr. A. had his worries. Now that his good friend Dulles was gone the West might start thinking of deals behind his back. Macmillan had been running between Washington and Moscow like Good Fairy Compromise. Ike had had Mr. K. as

PILOT THAT WON'T BE DROPPED

house-guest to the United States and was himself invited to pay a return visit to the Soviet Union. What would come of that? What was the influence of Macmillan on Ike, or vice versa? New U.S. Secretary of State Herter had just given his ideas on "co-survival". Adenauer had never been one for "co" ideas. All the same, a slice of luck had turned up. He had a new friend, de Gaulle, whose yearning for a French renaissance of prestige had made France adventurous and unpredictable and opened up new fields of manoeuvre. Who knew what possibilities of a powerful political "Little Europe" (eventually led by immortal Adenauer) might lie, for instance, in the Six States of the Common Market? True, some complications came with de Gaulle. He dreamed of a revival of the old-time link between Catholic Poland and Catholic France, which might not suit Germany.

And he had had a row with America about his rights concerning NATO nuclear weapons stored in France, causing America to redeploy nine fighter-bomber squadrons, some to Federal Germany. Britain and France had both played their foreign policy so clumsily that by contrast Federal Germany had begun to look like the only reliable member of NATO, and Adenauer America's No. 1 boy in Europe. On the whole, the situation was in hand.

THE ADAMANT SMILE

The Fifth Republic

De Gaulle had asked for six months. He began with Austerity, devalued the franc, raised taxes, cut subsidies and pensions. The real business of the régime began when with dictatorial powers he and M. Debré worked out a new constitution which took from the Assembly and gave to the President the power to make or unmake the governments of France. Having thus ended—on paper, at any rate— the chronic instability of French parliamentary life, he put his Constitution to a national referendum, on a plain *yes* or *no*. The French, stunned by the novel spectacle of a politician who knew his own mind, voted. The result was a vast resounding *yes*. A gaping world waited to see Superman start on the job of repairs he was put there for—Algeria . . . The issue upon which previous governments had foundered was, of course, autonomy or integration. The revolution which had carried him to power had originated at Algiers among the civil "Ultras" and military Blimps favouring total integration with France ("*Algérie Française!*"). They thought of de Gaulle as their man, as the man who would save the French Union (now the French Community) from the damned politicians if he had to blow it up in the attempt. No more negotiations for them. It was something of a shock, therefore, when de Gaulle, before even he was comfortably installed as President with a Make-it-Yourself government, proceeded to break up the inner nest of revolt, the Algiers Central Committee of Public Safety, by ordering all officers to withdraw from politics and mind their own military business; and followed that by shuffling those Generals who had become heroes of the "revolution" into other jobs. The atmosphere being now more salubrious for the Algerian Policy, it went on the air: extensive clemency for Algerian Nationalist prisoners; coupled with more military efficiency in continuing "pacification"; an offer to discuss a cease-fire; and political talks, but these would have to be preceded by surrender. (Surrender is so *final*,

THE PLIGHT OF THE PACIFIST

thought the rebels). The rebel Algerians would send duly elected Muslim representatives as deputies to speak for the nationalist cause at Paris. The nationalists kept mum. As a surprise kept for the last, the offer of a referendum in Algeria on a choice of secession, "Francisation" or federation. But pacification must come first. The rebel Algerian Provisional Government heard but still kept mum. (Pacification might mean cutting their throats.) Too much depended on de Gaulle's interpretation of the word "secession". They could not believe it meant that the Ultras, the Blimps, the die-hard settlers in Algeria were all going quietly back to France. As for the Ultras, the Blimps, the die-hards, they were outraged and began to throw stones. It was evident that this was a serial story to be continued in our next.

China and India

China's story was that everybody, including the Dalai Lama, was happy when the troops of the Chinese "motherland" arrived at Tibet. The effect was spoiled when the Dalai Lama made a dash for freedom and after a thrilling pursuit through mountain wilds escaped by way of the North-east Frontier Agency across the boundary into India. The Chinese authorities, with dreadful "lost face", said he must have been abducted. No Indian government could refuse a Dalai Lama political asylum. He was already the object of popular sympathy and now became the centre of pro-Tibetan agitation. It became a matter of political necessity for Peking to accuse India of complicity in Tibetan resistance, and to start up a violent press and

OPENING ROUND

radio campaign against all things Indian. Nehru patiently denied any hostility of Indians towards Chinese, but could not move from the obvious truth that India had a religious and cultural interest in Tibet. Unable to find a convincing reply to that, Chinese abuse rose an octave, and dilated upon the dangers to the Chinese of living next door to such a warmongering neighbour, and the sheer necessity of taking steps in self-defence. Prime Minister Chou En-lai declared that China had never ratified the Convention of 1914 whereby the "McMahon line" boundary had been established, so the so-called frontier wasn't binding. Maps were circulated including the whole Himalayan range from Ladakh to Assam in Chinese territory; Ladakh, Sukkim and Bhutan were shown as parts of Tibet. A wave of popular indignation swept India and the situation degenerated. It looked as though Nehru's pacifist fortitude would be put to a supreme test as Chou turned on the heat and armed clashes began up at the rocky frontier posts. As the decade ended the uncommitted East waited.

Ups and Downs in Space

1958 had ended with an American satellite functioning as a radio station reflecting and transmitting messages in outer space. Soviet scientists already led by several satellites in the competition for the Conquest of the Universe, and played up a moon rocket they launched at the beginning of 1959 as establishing the superiority of communism over capitalism. But Krushchev at the 20th Congress of the Soviet Communist Party had to admit that even at the end of the seven-year plan the Soviet Union would be behind leading capitalist countries in energy production and that the Russians could not catch up American industry for twelve years. In October, when a Russian rocket actually did hit the moon, the Americans had an attack of the horrors about the missiles gap, but they decided they still would have a substantial general superiority through the 1960's.

LUNAR DARTS

Never had it so Good

Britain's policy was how to combine monetary stability with rising standards and expanding production, reported Tribunals, Commissions and Councils. So the Government tried depressing the economy and cutting both living standards and investment. Then it struck the

OUTLOOK FOR THE CROPS

OUT ON A LIMB

Treasury that if the recession in America continued, it would bring a recession, very serious indeed, to Britain also, because protracted deflationary policies had left British economy precious little room to manoeuvre. So the Government, stagnant, changed its policy to Hope. As if to prove the British are the favoured of Providence, the outside world responded. The United States got over its recession, exports picked up, the balance of payments showed a surplus. After a popular Budget which put £365 millions back into spending money, Macmillan could hardly help winning the general election in November. Gad, this was PROSPERITY. Eat, drink and be merry, for the 'Sixties could look after themselves.

Labour Re-Thinking

After three electoral defeats in a row questions were asked within the Labour Party: Why had Labour lost its appeal? Was its programme out-of-date? "We must re-think our programme" said leader Gaitskell and his friends. Material prosperity had made the concepts of Marx as old-fashioned as his beard. They must move with the times, translate the principles laid down forty years ago into the needs of practical politics for the years ahead. The existing constitution was narrow and misleading, it said nothing about colonial freedom, race relations, disarmament, full employment planning, social equality. It harped too much on Clause 4, which was an election-loser. Even before mention of Clause 4 there was passionate dissent from the Party fundamentalists, who revered the constitution as Holy Writ, its virtue in the letter as much as in the spirit. They had clamoured against Gaitskell ever since he had taken over from Attlee as a man inclined too much to the Right (which was Right and which was Left could be discussed later): and now here he was uprooting sacred Clause 4 to prove it. "Public ownership of the means of production, distribution and exchange" had been good enough for their grandfathers and it was good enough for them, regardless of any change that might have come about since in the conditions of production, distribution and exchange. To substitute a new slogan "Control over the Economy" for the good old broad "Nationalisation" with its vague threat to the black hearts of the propertied classes was positively immoral. A clincher of a reason was advanced for dropping the whole subject. Theological argument would split the party. The rank-and-file had got used to the word "Nationalisation", however much they disagreed about its meaning. An egghead debate continued into the 'Sixties about definitions of Socialism, whether it was an ethical view, a certain way of life, a parcel of certain moral values or just the Good Society; what constituted the most suitable means for achieving it (avoiding identification of the Means with the End); and whether the Party objectives should be short or long—that is to say, should they point to a glorious millennium or at everybody being better off twenty years hence, or even just at the Labour Party winning the next election.

Peaceful Exploitation of Space

At close of play for the 'Fifties the Russians had hit the moon and also circled it, photographing its blind side and sending the result to

THE SMALL BOY IN US

earth by radio. The Americans had missed the moon but had photographed the sun and Venus from high altitude balloons. Both had fired animals into upper space, but no man. The Americans conceded to the Russians more powerful booster rockets of greater thrust, but claimed superiority in instrumentation and electronics, giving them a larger accumulation of space data, and a wider coverage of actual scientific discovery. The competitive aim in the 'Sixties would be to put into space a reconnaissance satellite to tell about weather, navigation, missile-warning and communication . . . Meanwhile legalists worried at the new problems that would certainly be created and ought to be controlled by supranational authority. In 1957 the subject of Peaceful Exploitation of Space had come up for discussion at the United Nations, but the Russians had bracketed "international co-operation in the study of cosmic space" with "foreign bases and military purposes", the Americans countered by bringing up "inspection", and nobody got anywhere. Various bodies and institutions had produced a protocol, and several conventions, to say pontifically that all States have complete and exclusive sovereignty over the air space above their territories. But they all forgot to define "air space". How do you decide the celestial frontier of a State's third-dimensional sovereignty? And the legal status of the space beyond that? How high does a landowner's ceiling reach? How can a householder prosecute someone for building a manned space station in his sky? And who takes third-party risks?

The Domestic Scene

On the home front 1959 was a year of Culture. Sir Winston Churchill's paintings at the Royal Academy drew more visitors than five previous exhibitions of Old Masters put together. Churchill refrained from the obvious comment . . . Plans for rebuilding part of Piccadilly Circus were published, but were found not to accord with Nash's colonnade . . . Laws were passed on prostitution and homosexuality, observing the principle that there is one morality for women, another for men . . . A new Minister of Transport planned a non-parking area, to be called the Pink Zone. He contemplated also a Blue Zone. Later he was seen to have turned pale green . . . The first speed road, M.1, was opened. Probably to demonstrate the superiority of feet, a lady walked from Edinburgh to London . . . 2,250 million pound notes circulated in Christmas shopping.

Epilogue

When speculators upon the future stick their necks out they nearly always dislocate their reputations. George Orwell's premonition of a sewn-up totalitarian world in 1984, and Aldous Huxley's anticipation of a grotesque life led by survivors of World War III will probably be as far out as Olaf Stapledon's imagination (in 1930) of a Europe unified by fear of America and her satellite, Russia, and H. G. Wells' dream (in 1933) of a United States unable to take part

ABOLITION OF MAN-LABOUR.— Big Boys of Atomic Industry stalled by problem of finding customers to keep the wheels turning.

THE PRESS-BUTTON AGE —1

in World War II. This is enough to show that oracles should practise humility and use plenty of "ifs" and "buts". A chain of reasoning may be sound enough, but things hardly ever run to logical conclusions in this world because of the eccentricity of human behaviour. Man himself is unreliable and not to be calculated. When prophets foretell the worst, their clients have always the chance of a pleasant surprise if things turn out well (as they frequently do, since Man cannot be depended upon even to make a fool of himself).

"Coming events cast their shadows before", but in a changing light, too many shadows perhaps. Prophets may deduce, for example, from current trends in co-operation, co-recreation and co-existence generally, that the Man of to-morrow must be a more harmonious creature than the Man of to-day; while to other prophets the prevailing inclination to live in one another's pockets, as expressed in clubs, societies, groups and gangs, could as convincingly point to a weakening of individualism and loss of the ability to stand alone. Does the achievement by Woman of political and economic equality with Man, together with the alleviation by science of her handicap of child-bearing, promise an increased fitness for the functions of wife and mother of the race? It as surely portends a progressive strengthening of confidence and character, which, taken with her appropriation of skills, sports, customs and modes of dress traditionally regarded as masculine, suggest a future in which Woman will be the pursuer, Man the pursued. More clearly foreshadowed is the Child of the future, as much the progeny of the Welfare authorities as of its parents. Times are approaching in which the control of population both as to quantity and quality, pre-natal selection and post-natal conditioning will be so definitely the business of the authorities as to silence argument. Without doubt the expansion of Welfare is to be read in all the signs and signals: the prevention or cure of illness, major or minor; added duration of life, with corresponding arrest of senility (as compensation, state-aided euthanasia for unwilling

PROBLEM OF LEISURE: Presentation of the GOLD PICK to winners of jobs in 1st. Battalion, Heroes of Labour.

THE PRESS-BUTTON AGE — 2

reactionaries); and, among a spate of medical and surgical innovations of, say, the year 2100, the availability of human spare parts.

Science is secretive, so one can only conjecture what it has in store. Weather control, of course. Highly improved communications, no doubt—something in the way of individual flying devices, safe, noiseless and clean. Labour abolishing contrivances ad infinitum. Vast innovations in Entertainment—life-sized 3-dimensional singers, comedians and dancers built out of light, without the need for those cumbersome radio and TV boxes. Who will bother with newspapers when one can see, hear, smell and feel the news as it happens? Who will read novels when one can listen to the latest Homer, with one's wristwatch-size recorder to fix him for repeat and re-repeat as desired? The augmenting of food reserves by copious supplies of delicious plankton from the seas. (What the fish will live on will also receive attention, no doubt.) Domestic central heating piped from the boiling underworld. Pleasure cruises to the interior of the earth, to the floor of the seas, to the stars. (The moon will be small stuff, a boring place by the look of it.) New powers, new energies, yes, yes. We have not begun on the Sun yet.

The future potential of Science fires imagination to exceed the speed limit. The political future is to be approached more cautiously, because of the imponderables and unpredictables of personality and leadership. Unfortunately the picture of superman Ministers, primed by their departmental experts, embassies, spies and agents, planning five moves ahead and directing gigantic operations with cool efficiency is less like the truth than that suggested by diaries and State papers of harassed and confused fellow creatures sitting on the edges of their beds in the middle of the night wondering what to do next that will checkmate their foreign opponents and at the same time square with their political situations at home. Frequently they do things which are unaccountable.

The threads of the 'Fifties continue into the 'Sixties, the 'Seventies, the 'Eighties. . . . On the very doorstep sit four unpredictables. Dr. Adenauer, President de Gaulle, Generalissimo Chiang Kai-shek, Pandit Nehru, aged monuments of dedicated personal rule, each the personification of a disputed but stubbornly held idea. None is immortal, and when in due course they depart, each will leave a large hole and the probability of change. Thus a cautious oracle in 1960 labouring under this formidable handicap, might assume pink spectacles after a hearty breakfast and try to estimate the future of, say, Europe, by all the lights of past experience and present tendencies, making reasonable allowance at least for alternative courses of events.

A final polish on its industrial machine, and Soviet Russia will open the new phase of economic assault to undercut the capitalist countries in their world markets. With the "Six" and the "Seven" evolving eventually into a political European Federation, including

Britain (by special arrangement with the Commonwealth) and with strings to the United States, the Russian Question would thus be met with a European Answer. A strengthened and more confident West could afford to play bluff poker with Moscow. Trade barriers are never absolute, and sooner or later, bargaining under various pressures and persuasions, would unify the two Germanies at a price of a face-saving Polish frontier accommodation and a duplex political organisation, neither communist nor anti-communist. Through the association of Germany with the company of ex-"satellites" (re-labelled) of the Warsaw Pact (consolidated with NATO) new patterns would emerge in both Eastern and Western Europe. Ideologies, too, evolve. A new generation of Russians, six generations away from Lenin, apprehensive of China, and even in the late 'Fifties showing palpable signs of "flexibility" and "embourgeoise-ment", could do business with a new generation of Germans,

PRESSURE of PRODUCTION —
Compulsory exports for the backward peoples.

THE PRESS-BUTTON AGE —3

Frenchmen and Britons bored with "politics" and always willing to leave the responsibilities of democracy to leaders. There would be an historic occasion at Geneva when the two sides, grown much less distinguishable, meet one another half-way to a golden age. At a trade summit promoted by the United States resources would be planned, the needs of the under-supplied peoples would be satisfied. This would be the Era of the Businessman. The Age of Materialism would have produced its fruit. The hard-headed "realists" would rule and "idealists" would be execrated and hide their heads.

This might happen. On the other hand, it might not. Change pink spectacles for blue and look on this alternative: the attenuation of NATO (on grounds of economy, in the belief that the best security against war is to remain solvent); the withdrawal from Europe of the United States to cope with the, by then, more important peril of China; a crisis over Germany coming dangerously near to war, and the German Problem finally solved on Soviet terms. The addition of all Western Europe (including Britain) to the company of satellites in the new ETO (European Treaty Organisation) might well break the Soviet Union. At the very least it would set the stage for a hundred years of new groupings and groups within groupings. Again the planned resources and productive machines would compel by circumstances a higher standard of material well-being. Another golden age, with some important differences in detail. So long as the United States could be held off separate and apart to be represented, for internal political purposes, as "the imperialist aggressor", foreign policy and defence would be above local interference and under rigid control of the Central Executive. Britain's geographical position would make it naturally the forward rocket base.

Confucius held that in times of stress one should take short views— only up to lunchtime. The writer has glanced at to-day and to-morrow, leaving the day after to others. No mention of the Chinese Age, the

Indian Era or the African Millennium, much less of the distant
European Renaissance in the United States of Australia. Each will
have its long—too long—unfolding story with its periods of wellbeing
and illbeing, joys and sorrows, peace and war.

Neither has the writer touched until now on war (a tender subject
upon which civilised man is tempted to deceive himself), except to
take for granted over the centuries its recurrent probabilities, with
or without limitations. The signing of agreements or the ceremonious
scrapping of weapons can at best do no more than ensure peace for
limited periods. Now that Man has the know-how of vast destruction,
he is not likely to forget it; and it would be unduly optimistic to
suppose that, as time rolls on, while Science remains obligingly in
status quo, somewhere, sometime, someone will not break the com-
parative security of a gentleman's agreement and press the button.
But it would be unduly pessimistic, on the other hand, to suppose
that Science has made its last contribution to history. It is no more
unreasonable to expect a counter to the H-bomb than it would have
been fifty years ago to expect to rocket to the moon. Science will have
new wonders in its task of reducing war to an absurdity. Having
already perfected explosives that shiver the heaviest armour to
fragments, and airplanes so fast as to make combat impossible, we
may hope they will pass on to a magnetic force, perhaps, that will
boomerang missiles so that they turn in flight and whistle back to
where they came from; or an inplosion (forced contraction of air)
which may be fired at an explosion (forced expansion of air) to
neutralise it and keep atmospheric normality. Certainly there will be
a Ray, that masterpiece of the future that will make the obsolete
H-bomb look like a clumsy toy.

War, like some other matters, must await a supranational or
world authority. Meanwhile various knotty problems already
familiar in their shaping, will insist on solution. The wages system
will have been dislocated by automatic production. Management of

industry will be stalled by the problem of finding customers to keep
the wheels turning. One can imagine a conference of Government,
Management and Welfare authorities to worry about the reaching
of saturation point in the home market. The devices for welfare
distribution of purchasing power are exhausted. How to turn possible
consumers into probable customers? The conference will decide to
distribute, say, motor-cars free to everybody on Compulsory Perpetual
"Never-never". The Powers (under stress of emergency all artificial
political differences will have disappeared) will insist on supplying
the last obstinate "backward peoples" with the blessings of civilisation—or else.

With man-labour reduced to a minimum, a second problem will
demand attention: leisure. The superfluous ex-workers will get sick
of football, horse-racing and dancing. To prevent moral rot, the
welfare authorities will plan to occupy them with gigantic glamorous
jobs like damming the Mediterranean to water the Sahara, building
a mountain in Central Australia to catch the rain; installing space
stations to control the seasons. These jobs will carry much prestige.
The Pride of Work will be rediscovered.

It is unlikely that the blessings of A.D. 2200 will run smoothly
without a considerable measure of Order, that is to say, without a
cost to the citizens of restricted freedom of expression, information,
association and movement. The system will be, of course, still
"democracy" and after eight generations people will be so used to it
that they will not know what you will be talking about when you
complain that democracy is not what it used to be. There will be
the democratic institutions of Parliament (with slight adjustment
concerning freedom of choice) and two-party representation, the
Party of Order and the Party of Freedom—the former placing
emphasis on the discipline necessary to the maintenance of a luxurious
standard of life, the latter placing emphasis on the need for applying
as much of the spiritual values as the circumstances allow.

The conflict of ideas, the integration of bodies of doctrine, the building of better societies; the universe to play with; expeditions to the unexplored regions of the mind—even to the source of life itself; the endless conflict between wisdom and stupidity, reason and prejudice, greed and charity, love and hate. . . . Would you want a life without peril? That you will never get. As the old Chinese philosopher remarked: "If it's not one thing it's another. It's never Nothing". For which we should be truly thankful.